Bright Lights AND Shadowy Shapes

by Jennifer Waters

Content and Reading Adviser: Joan Stewart
Educational Consultant/Literacy Specialist
New York Public Schools

Spyglass BOOKS

COMPASS POINT BOOKS

Minneapolis, Minnesota

Compass Point Books
3722 West 50th Street, #115
Minneapolis, MN 55410

Visit Compass Point Books on the Internet at *www.compasspointbooks.com*
or e-mail your request to *custserv@compasspointbooks.com*

Photographs ©:
Two Coyote Studios/Mary Walker Foley, cover; PhotoDisc, 4, 5; Two Coyote Studios/Mary Walker Foley, 6;
PhotoDisc, 7; Two Coyote Studios/Mary Walker Foley, 8, 9, 11, 12; Visuals Unlimited/Bill Banaszewski, 13;
Stock Montage, 14; Two Coyote Studios/Mary Walker Foley, 15, 16, 17, 18, 19, 21.

Project Manager: Rebecca Weber McEwen
Editor: Alison Auch
Photo Researcher: Jennifer Waters
Photo Selectors: Rebecca Weber McEwen and Jennifer Waters
Designer: Mary Walker Foley

Library of Congress Cataloging-in-Publication Data

Waters, Jennifer.
  Bright lights and shadowy shapes / by Jennifer Waters.
     p. cm. -- (Spyglass books)
Includes bibliographical references and index.
  ISBN 0-7565-0227-6 (hardcover)
 1. Shades and shadows--Juvenile literature. [1. Light. 2. Shadows.]
I. Title. II. Series.
  QA519 .W28 2002
  535'.4--dc21
                              2001007332

14047

Contents

Stars

Stars are big balls of *gas* that give off heat and light.

The sun is the closest star to Earth.

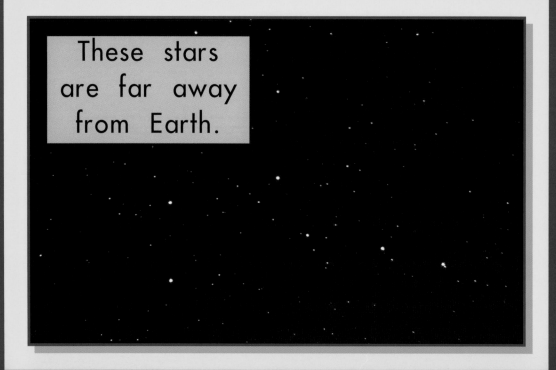

These stars are far away from Earth.

Shadows

It is dark at night because one side of Earth is turned away from the sun. This makes a huge shadow over that side of Earth.

When the moon moves
in front of the sun, it makes
a shadow over Earth.
This is called an *eclipse*.

What Makes a Shadow?

If an object blocks light from shining through, the dark area that the light cannot reach is a shadow.

Your Shadow

The size of your shadow changes during the day.

Shadows are smallest at *midday*.
Early or late in the day, shadows are long and thin.
At night, there are no shadows.

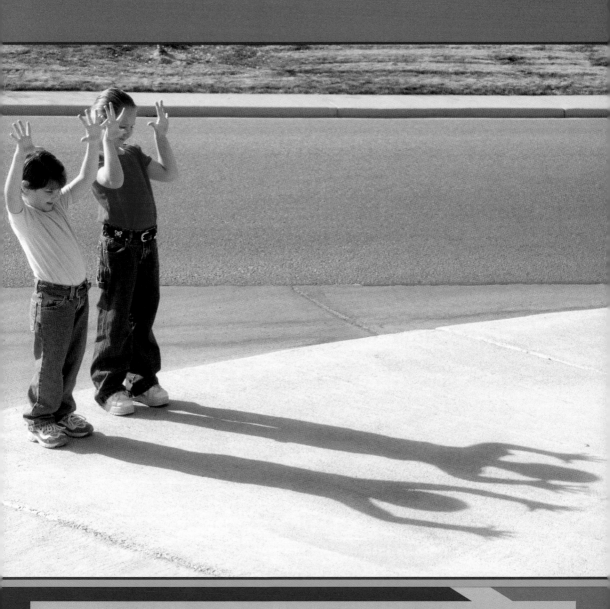

When the sun is low in the sky,
a shadow is long.

Before the Lightbulb

Long ago, people used *torches* and small fires that burned in big shells or stones.

Later, people used candles and oil-burning lamps to see at night.

A candle

A campfire

13

The Lightbulb

Thomas Alva Edison invented the lightbulb in 1879. Back then, most people did not have electricity. Not many people could use lightbulbs.

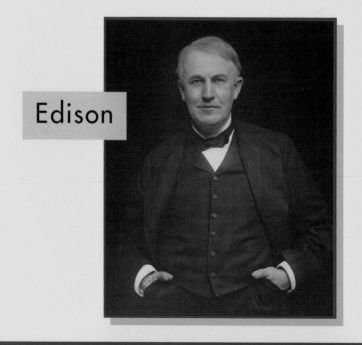

Edison

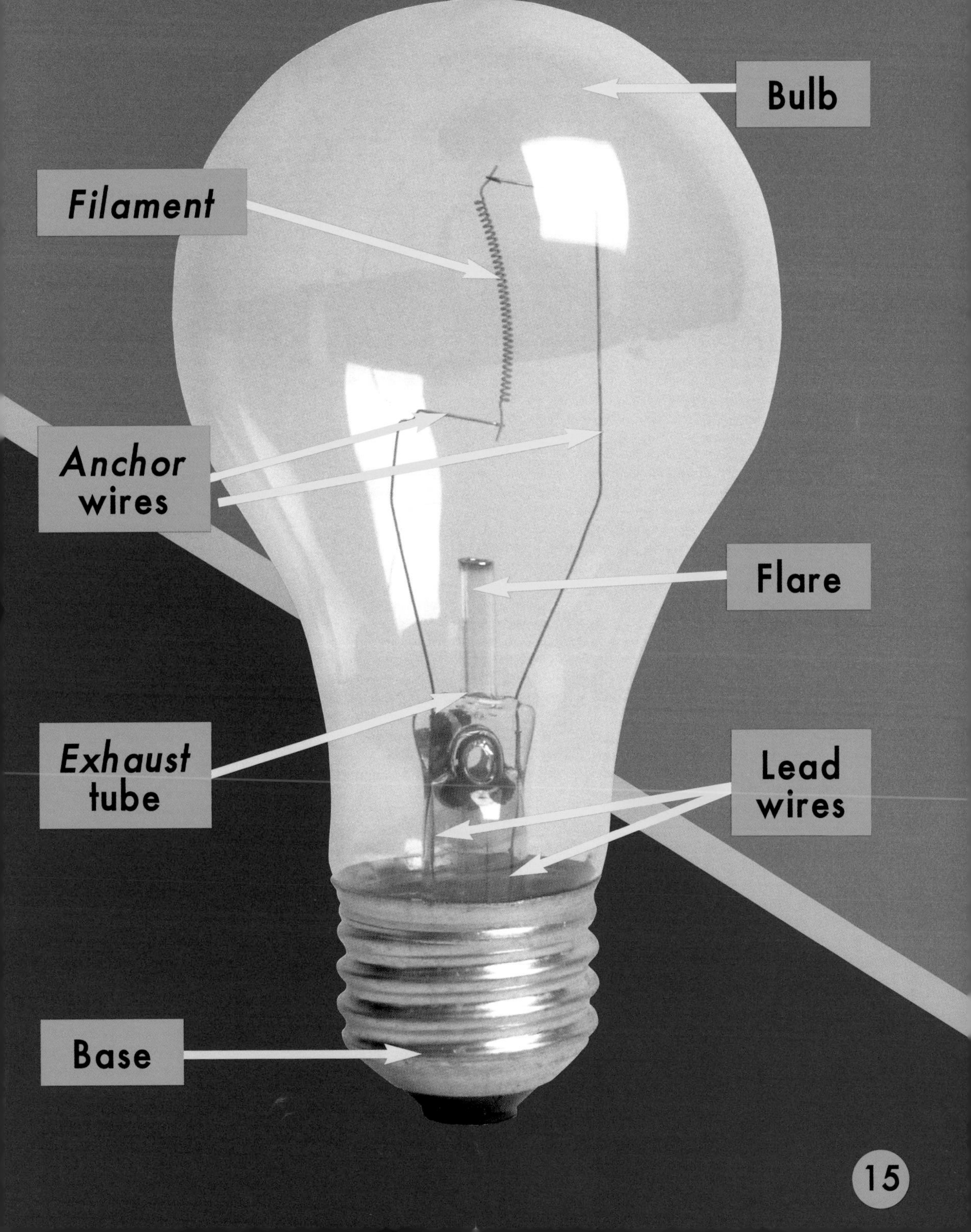

Bulb

Filament

Anchor
wires

Flare

Exhaust
tube

Lead
wires

Base

Shadow Puppets

People who watch
shadow puppet shows see
shadows, not the puppets.

Shadow puppets are flat.
They move behind a screen,
and there is always
a bright light shining
from behind them.

Guess These Shadows

Can you guess what is making these shadows?

Make your own shadows and quiz your friends.

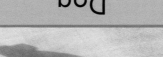

Lamp

Dog

Cat

Fun Facts

People used to believe that if a groundhog sees its shadow on Groundhog Day (February 2), there will be six more weeks of winter.

People in the Far East
have enjoyed watching
shadow puppet plays
for thousands of years.

Glossary

anchor—an object that holds something in one place

eclipse—when one object in space blocks light and keeps it from shining on another object in space

exhaust—something that pulls a gas out of something else

filament—a very thin thread or wire

gas—a substance that does not have an exact shape or size

midday—the middle of the day, when the sun is overhead

torches—hand-held pieces of wood that are lit with fire at one end

Learn More

Books

Baxter, Nicola. *Living with Light.*
  Chicago: Childrens Press, 1996.

Branley, Franklyn M. *Day Light, Night
  Light: Where Light Comes From.* New
  York: HarperCollins, 1998.

Bulla, Clyde Robert. *What Makes a
  Shadow?* Illustrated by June Otani.
  New York: HarperCollins, 1994.

Web Site

Brain Pop
www.brainpop.com/science/seeall.weml
  (click on "eclipse," "light," or "sun")

Index

GR: H
Word Count: 176

From Jennifer Waters

I live near the Rocky Mountains.
The ocean is my favorite place.
I like to write songs and books.
I hope you enjoyed this book.